To:

_____

From:

_____

Date:

_____

Be My Valentine

Celebrating the Gift of Love

HONOR
B O O K S

07 06 05 04 03   10 9 8 7 6 5 4 3 2 1

Be My Valentine
Celebrating the Gift of Love
ISBN 1-56292-003-0
Copyright © 2003 by Honor Books
An Imprint of Cook Communications Ministries
P.O. Box 55388
Tulsa, Oklahoma 74155

Compiled by Betsy Williams

Introduction

Celebrated since the Middle Ages, Valentine's Day has been dedicated to many forms and expressions of love. Its specific origins are unknown, but one legend tells of a Christian priest named Valentine, imprisoned and soon to be martyred for his faith. He wrote a farewell letter to the daughter of his jailer and signed it "From Your Valentine." If true, his one small, loving act has endured to this day as a lasting symbol of love.

Be My Valentine is designed to inspire your Valentine's Day celebration in the tradition of Saint Valentine. We have filled it with poems, quotes, scriptures and stories. We hope as you move through the pages, you will embrace the gift Saint Valentine left for us all.

With love,
Honor Books

*T*he greatest pleasure of life is love.

—Sir William Temple

♥ ♥ ♥

Now these three remain: faith, hope and love.
But the greatest of these is love.

1 Corinthians 13:13

A Love Story from the Bible

The LORD God said, "It is not good for the man to be alone. I will make a helper suitable for him." So the LORD God caused the man to fall into a deep sleep; and while he was sleeping, he took one of the man's ribs and closed up the place with flesh. Then the LORD God made a woman from the rib he had taken out of the man, and he brought her to the man.

The man said,

> *"This is now bone of my bones*
> *and flesh of my flesh;*
> *she shall be called 'woman,'*
> *for she was taken out of man."*

For this reason a man will leave his father and mother and be united to his wife, and they will become one flesh.

Genesis 2:18, 21–25

The Most Wonderful Thing

The most wonderful of all things in life,
I believe, is the discovery of another human being
with whom one's relationship has a glowing depth, beauty,
and joy as the years increase.
This inner progressiveness of love between two human beings
is a most marvelous thing;
it cannot be found by looking for it
or by passionately wishing for it.
It is a sort of Divine accident.

—Sir Hugh Walpole

*M*any things in life will catch your eye,
but only a few will catch your heart.

—Author Unknown

♥ ♥ ♥

The LORD does not look at the things man looks at. Man looks
at the outward appearance, but the LORD looks at the heart.

1 Samuel 16:7

God's Beautiful Dream of Love

By wisdom a house is built,
and through understanding it is established;
through knowledge its rooms are filled
with rare and beautiful treasures.

Proverbs 24:3–4

*L*ove in marriage should be the accomplishment of a beautiful dream.

—Jean Baptiste Alphonse Karr

Some Day

I know not when the day shall be,
I know not when our eyes may meet;
What welcome you may give to me,
Or will your words be sad or sweet,

It may not be 'till years have passed,
'Till eyes are dim and tresses gray;
The world is wide, but, love, at last,
Our hands, our hearts, must meet some day.

—Hugh Conway

Kiss a Day

A West German magazine reported the results of a study conducted by a life insurance company. The researchers discovered that husbands who kiss their wives every morning enjoy the following benefits:

- ♥ They live an average of five years longer,
- ♥ They are involved in fewer automobile accidents,
- ♥ They are ill 50 percent less, as noted by sick days, and
- ♥ They earn 20 to 30 percent more money.

Other researchers found that kissing and hugging release endorphins, giving mind and body a sense of genuine well-being that is translated into better health.

A kiss a day may just keep the doctor away!

[The kiss] is as old as the creation,
and yet as young and fresh as ever.
It pre-existed, still exists, and always will exist.
Depend upon it,
Eve learned it in Paradise, and was taught
its beauties, virtues, and varieties by an angel,
there is something so transcendent in it.

—Thomas C. Haliburton

A Note from Me to You

When I look back at how God brought us together,
I marvel at His timing and the way He arranged it all.
And then we fell in love . . . what a mystery indeed!
Out of all the people in the world, you are the one
He chose for me. I love His choice; I love you.

The ways of the heart, like the ways of providence, are mysterious.

—Henry Ware

♥ ♥ ♥

There are three things too wonderful for me to understand—no, four!
How an eagle glides through the sky.
How a serpent crawls upon a rock.
How a ship finds its way across the heaving ocean.
The growth of love between a man and a girl.

Proverbs 30:18–19 TLB

A Very Special Day

The fourteenth of February is a day sacred to St. Valentine!
It was a very odd notion, alluded to by Shakespeare,
that on this day birds begin to couple; hence, perhaps,
arose the custom of sending on this day letters
containing professions of love and affection.

—Noah Webster

Did you know?

The oldest known valentine in existence was sent by Charles, Duke of Orleans to his wife while he was imprisoned in the Tower of London in 1415. This valentine is currently stored at the British Library in London, England.

Kisses Are Wonderful

It is the passion that is in a kiss that gives to it its sweetness;
it is the affection in a kiss that sanctifies it.

—Christian Nestell Bovee

et him kiss me with the kisses of his mouth—
for your love is more delightful than wine.
Pleasing is the fragrance of your perfumes;
your name is like perfume poured out.

Song of Songs 1:2–3

23

Waiting for Daisy

The girls gradually came out on to the lawn. I began to fear that Daisy was not coming. She was the last of all. I was horribly afraid she had been advised not to appear, because I was there. Presently I turned and there she was in a black velvet jacket and light dress, with a white feather in her hat and her bright golden hair tied up with blue riband. How bright and fresh and happy and pretty she looked.

I love her more and more each time I see her. I think she loves me a little. I hope so. God grant it. I am sure she does not dislike me, and I believe, I do believe, she likes me and cares for me. I fancy I can see it in her clear loving deep grey eyes, so true and fearless and honest, those beautiful Welsh eyes that seem to like to meet mine. I think she likes to be with me and talk with me, or why did she come back to me again and again and stand by me and talk to no one else? I wish I could tell her how dearly I love her but I dare not.

—The Reverend Francis Kilvert

Mutual Love

The plainest man that can convince a woman that
he is really in love with her, has done more to make
her in love with him than the handsomest man,
if he can produce no such conviction.
For the love of woman is a shoot, not a seed, and
flourishes most vigorously only when ingrafted on
that love which is rooted in the breast of another.

—Caleb C. Colton

*M*utual love is the crown of all our bliss.

—John Milton

♥ ♥ ♥

Love comes from God and those who are loving and kind show that they are the children of God.

1 John 4:7 TLB

He Willed that We Should Meet

Love took you by the hand
At eve, and bade you stand
At edge of the woodland,
Where I should pass;
Love sent me thither, sweet,
And brought me to your feet;
He willed that we should meet,
And so it was.

—John Bowyer Buchanan Nichols

*Every good and perfect gift is from above,
coming down from the Father of the heavenly lights,
who does not change like shifting shadows.*

James 1:17

A Beautiful Love Story

Harry S. Truman first met his future bride, Bess, in Sunday school when he was six and she was just five. "She had golden curls and beautiful blue eyes," he remembered fondly. Although they graduated from high school together in 1901, the paths of their lives led in different directions until nine years later when they became reacquainted. "I thought she was the most beautiful and the sweetest person on earth," he later shared of their reunion.

From that point on, Harry began courting Bess, in part through written letters. Even after they married nine years later, the two continued their correspondence through fifty-three years of marriage, including their years in the White House. Although most of Bess's letters have been lost to history, more than thirteen hundred of Harry's missives have survived in the Truman Library collections.

Thine Am I, My Faithful Fair

What is life, when wanting love?
Night without a morning;
Love's the cloudless summer sun,
Nature gay adorning.

—Robert Burns

How Many Times

How many times do I love again?
Tell me how many beads there are
In a silver chain
Of evening rain
Unravelled from the trembling main
And threading the eye of a yellow star—
So many times do I love again.

—Thomas Lovell

The Sweetness of Your Lips

You have stolen my heart, my sister, my bride;
you have stolen my heart
with one glance of your eyes,
with one jewel of your necklace.
How delightful is your love, my sister, my bride!
How much more pleasing is your love than wine,
and the fragrance of your perfume than any spice!
Your lips drop sweetness as the honeycomb, my bride;
milk and honey are under your tongue.

Song of Songs 4:9–11

*F*our sweet lips, two pure souls,
and one undying affection—
these are love's pretty ingredients for a kiss.

—Christian Nestell Bovee

35

A Note from Me to You

There are so many things I love about you: the way your eyes sparkle when you laugh, the sound of your voice, the gentleness of your touch, and the passion of your kiss. There's no one else in all the world that could ever take your place. You're one of a kind, and I'm glad that you're mine.

*N*othing more excites to all
that is noble and generous,
than virtuous love.

—Henry Home

Did you know?

There are at least three different saints named Valentine or Valentinus, to whom our present-day holiday could be attributed, and all were martyred. Although historians disagree as to which one should be credited, one possibility is a Saint Valentine who was a Roman Catholic bishop put to death in Rome about AD 270. Legend has it that he went from door to door anonymously leaving food on the doorsteps of the poor. Many believe the custom of sending anonymous Valentine greetings developed from this practice.

*"When you give to the needy, do not let your left hand know what
your right hand is doing, so that your giving may be in secret.
Then your Father, who sees what is done in secret, will reward you."*

Matthew 6:3–4

♥ ♥ ♥

*T*he manner of giving shows the character
of the giver, more than the gift itself.

—John Caspar Lavater

39

True Love Is Sensitive to Others

Passion may be blind; but to say that love is,
is a libel and a lie.—
Nothing is more sharp-sighted or sensitive than true love,
in discerning, as by an instinct, the feelings of another.

—William Henry Davis

*You should be of one mind, full of
sympathy toward each other,
loving one another with tender hearts
and humble minds.*

1 Peter 3:8 NLT

Love Covers

Love covers a multitude of sins. When a scar cannot be taken away, the next kind office is to hide it.—Love is never so blind as when it is to spy faults.—It is like the painter, who . . . to draw the picture of a friend having a blemish in one eye, would picture only the other side of his face.

—Robert South

*As God's chosen ones, holy and beloved,
clothe yourselves with compassion, kindness,
humility, meekness, and patience.
Bear with one another.*

Colossians 3:12–13 NRSV

The Coming of Love

It seems to me that the coming of love is like the coming of spring—the date is not to be reckoned by the calendar. It may be slow and gradual; it may be quick and sudden. But in the morning, when we wake and recognize a change in the world without, verdure on the trees, blossoms on the sward, warmth in the sunshine, music in the air, we say spring has come.

—Edward George Bulwer-Lytton

My lover is radiant and ruddy,
outstanding among ten thousand.
His head is purest gold;
his hair is wavy
and black as a raven.
His eyes are like doves
by the water streams,
washed in milk,
mounted like jewels.

Song of Songs 5:10–12

A Beautiful Commitment

Two persons who have chosen each other out of all
the species, with the design to be each other's mutual
comfort and entertainment, have, in that action, bound
themselves to be good-humored, affable, discreet,
forgiving, patient, and joyful, with respect to each other's
frailties and perfections, to the end of their lives.

—Joseph Addison

*Commit everything you do to the LORD.
Trust him, and he will help you.*

Psalm 37:5 NLT

A Beautiful Love Story

The lives of Ronald and Nancy Reagan have been chronicled through their many years of public life and service. From his life as an actor, to their lives in the White House, and even to their current battle with Alzheimers, we have been privileged to watch them handle life's triumphs and tragedies with grace.

One of the most touching aspects of their lives is the beautiful and loving relationship they have cultivated through over fifty years of marriage. During the course of their journey together, Ronald has written volumes of charmingly romantic love letters to his bride. These letters offer an inside look at matters of the heart and can now be enjoyed by all through Nancy's book, *I Love You, Ronnie.*

Let's Grow Old Together

Grow old along with me!
The best is yet to be,
The last of life, for which the first was made:
Our times are in his hand,
Who saith, "A whole I planned,
Youth shows but half; trust God:
See all, nor be afraid!"

—Robert Browning

*M*emory, wit, fancy, acuteness,
cannot grow young again in old age;
but the heart can.

—Jean Paul Richter

♥ ♥ ♥

The glory of youths is their strength,
but the beauty of the aged
is their gray hair.

Proverbs 20:29 NRSV

Valentine's Day Around the World

In Great Britain, it is customary for children to sing special Valentine's Day songs and to receive gifts of money, candy, or fruit. In days gone by, the children of the town of Norfolk often played a game similar to tag in which the person tagged had to offer up a small token Valentine's gift.

Young suitors in the town of Norwich would secretly leave baskets of gifts on the doorsteps of their sweethearts, ringing the bell and running away to avoid discovery. Today, housewives in Rutland County customarily make special buns containing caraway seeds and plums or currants to mark the occasion.

*I*n every nation he has those who
worship him and do good deeds
and are acceptable to him.

Acts 10:35 TLB

A Note from Me to You

I believe in you. God made you just the way you are on purpose.
No one else possesses your unique combination of strengths, gifts,
and talents; and He designed you to succeed. As you seek Him first
and His plans for your life, I am confident He will prosper you in
all your ways. I'm here to support you; I love you very much.

I am confident of this very thing,
that He who began a good work in you
will perfect it until the day of Christ Jesus.

Philippians 1:6 NASB

♥ ♥ ♥

 man loved by a beautiful and virtuous woman,
carries with him a talisman that renders him invulnerable;
every one feels that such a one's life has
a higher value than that of others.

—Amantine Lucile Aurore Dudevant

I write this greeting in my own hand.

2 Thessalonians 3:17

*L*etters are those winged messengers
that can fly from east to west
on embassies of love.

—Jeremiah Brown Howell

Did you know?

Of the three possible Saint Valentines to whom the holiday could be attributed, legend holds that one of these men actually sent the first of these sentimental greetings himself. This saint was allegedly jailed and martyred for aiding persecuted Christians. While imprisoned, it is said that he healed his jailer's daughter of blindness and fell in love with her. Before he was put to death, he supposedly wrote her a letter, signing it "From Your Valentine"—an expression we still use today.

Kisses for All Occasions

There is the kiss of welcome and of parting;
the long, lingering, loving, present one;
the stolen, or the mutual one;
the kiss of love, of joy, and of sorrow;
the seal of promise and receipt of fulfillment.
Is it strange, therefore, that a woman
is invincible whose armory consists of
kisses, smiles, sighs, and tears?

—Thomas C. Haliburton

Love

Greet one another with a kiss of love.
Peace to all of you who are in Christ.

1 Peter 5:14

♥ ♥ ♥

*W*ith velvet lip, print on his brow
such language as tongue hath never spoken.

—Lydia H. Sigourney

Falling in Love

Young love-making, that gossamer web! Even the points it clings to—the things when its subtle interlacings are swung—are scarcely perceptible: momentary touches of finger-tips, meetings of rays from blue and dark orbs, unfinished phrases, lightest changes of cheek and lip, faintest tremors. The web itself is made of spontaneous beliefs and indefinable joys, yearnings of one life toward another, visions of completeness, indefinite trust.

—George Eliot

*ike an apple tree among the trees of the forest
is my lover among the young men.
I delight to sit in his shade,
and his fruit is sweet to my taste.*

Song of Songs 2:3

The Divine Plan of Love

*"A new command I give you: Love one another.
As I have loved you, so you must love one another.
By this all men will know that you are my disciples,
if you love one another."*

John 13:34–35

*A true friend is always loyal, and
a brother is born to help in time of need.*

Proverbs 17:17 TLB

♥ ♥ ♥

The greatest happiness of life is the conviction
that we are loved, loved for ourselves,
or rather loved in spite of ourselves.

—Victor Hugo

The Love Chapter

*Love is very patient and kind, never jealous
or envious, never boastful or proud, never haughty
or selfish or rude. Love does not demand its own way.
It is not irritable or touchy. It does not hold grudges
and will hardly even notice when others do it wrong.*

It is never glad about injustice, but rejoices whenever truth wins out.
If you love someone, you will be loyal to him no matter what the cost.
You will always believe in him, always expect the best of him,
and always stand your ground in defending him.

1 Corinthians 13:4–8 TLB

A White Rose

The red rose whispers of passion,
And the white rose breathes of love;
O, the red rose is a falcon,
And the white rose is a dove.

But I send you a cream-white rosebud
With a flush on its petal tips;
For the love that is purest and sweetest
Has a kiss of desire on the lips.

—John Boyle O'Reilly

Did you know?

Of the three saints named Valentine to whom the holiday could be attributed, one was a priest in Rome during the reign of Emperor Claudius II. In order to build up the Roman army, Claudius outlawed marriage for all young men, believing single men made better soldiers than those who were family men. Legend says that in defiance, Valentine continued to marry young lovers in secret until he was discovered and consequently put to death.

Completing One Another

He is the half part of a blessed man
Left to be finished by such as she;
And she a fair divided excellence,
Whose fullness of perfection lies in him.
O, two such silver currents, when they join,
Do glorify the banks that bound them in!

—Geoffrey Chaucer

No Longer Two, but One

"'For this reason a man will leave his father and mother and
be united to his wife, and the two will become one flesh.'
So they are no longer two, but one.
Therefore what God has joined together, let man not separate."

Mark 10:7–9

*T*rue love's the gift which God hath given,
to man alone beneath the heaven.
The silver link, the silver tie,
which heart to heart, and mind to mind,
in body and in soul can bind.

—Sir Walter Scott

*If one prevail against him, two shall withstand him;
and a threefold cord is not quickly broken.*

Ecclesiastes 4:12 KJV

♥ ♥ ♥

*B*lest be the tie that binds
Our hearts in Christian love;
The fellowship of kindred minds
Is like that to that above.

—Johann Georg Nägeli

A Note from Me to You

You are the one who's won my heart; you are the one for me.

I never cease to pray for you to fulfill your destiny.

You are the one that lights my fire, the one who makes my heart sing.

And every day I think of you as I wear my wedding ring.

You are the one who keeps me warm, when the world outside is cold.
Your glance still gives me chills and you are the one I love to hold.
I praise the Lord above for bringing you into my life and world.
And every day I'll treasure you, like a precious gem of pearl.

Valentine's Day Around the World

In some parts of Italy, people celebrate February 14
with Valentine's Day feasts. In Sicily it is customary
for young women to stand by their windows, for hours
sometimes, waiting for a young man to pass by.
It is their belief that within the year they will
marry this man or someone who looks like him.

Love

Look in the scroll of the LORD and read:
None of these will be missing,
not one will lack her mate.
For it is his mouth that has given the order,
and his Spirit will gather them together.

Isaiah 34:16

A Love Story from the Bible

*Laban had two daughters; the name of the older
was Leah, and the name of the younger was Rachel.
Leah had weak eyes, but Rachel was lovely in form, and beautiful.
Jacob was in love with Rachel and said, "I'll work for you
seven years in return for your younger daughter Rachel."*

*Laban said, "It's better that I give her to you than to some other man.
Stay here with me." So Jacob served seven years to get Rachel, but
they seemed like only a few days to him because of his love for her.*

Genesis 29:16–20

*The happy minglement of hearts, where,
changed as chemic compounds are,
each with its own existence parts,
to find a new one, happier far.*

—Thomas Moore

Genuine Love

Nothing quickens the perceptions like genuine love.
From the humblest professional attachment
to the most chivalric devotion,
what keenness of observation is born
under the influence of that feeling
which drives away the obscuring clouds of selfishness,
as the sun consumes the vapor of the morning.

—Henry Theodore Tuckerman

"*No one has greater love than this,*
to lay down one's life for one's friends."

John 15:13 NRSV

Joined for Life

What greater thing is there for two human souls
than to feel that they are joined for life—
to strengthen each other in all labor,
to rest on each other in all sorrow,
to minister to each other in all pain,
to be one with each other
in silent, unspeakable memories
at the moment of the last parting.

—George Eliot

*Two are better than one, because
they have a good reward for their toil.
For if they fall, one will lift up the other.*

Ecclesiastes 4:9–10 NRSV

The Most Generous of the Passions

Love is the most terrible,
and also the most generous of the passions;
it is the only one that includes in its dreams
the happiness of someone else.

—Jean Baptiste Alphonse Karr

Let no one seek his own, but each one the other's well-being.

1 Corinthians 10:24 NKJV

The Scent of Blessings

The treasures of the deep are not so
precious as are the concealed comforts
of a man locked up in woman's love:
I scent the air of blessings when
I come but near the house.

—Thomas Middleton

As far as God is concerned there is a sweet, wholesome fragrance in our lives. It is the fragrance of Christ within us, an aroma to both the saved and the unsaved all around us. To those who are not being saved, we seem a fearful smell of death and doom, while to those who know Christ we are a life-giving perfume.

2 Corinthians 2:15–16 TLB

We Are Equals in Christ

We are no longer Jews or Greeks or slaves or free men or even merely men or women, but we are all the same— we are Christians; we are one in Christ Jesus.

Galatians 3:28 TLB

Did you know?

Esther Howard is acknowledged as the first person to perfect the assembly-line method of card design in 1948. In a day when women regularly worked in factories for up to fifteen hours per day for little pay to create valentines, Ms. Howland was known for paying good wages to her female employees.

A Beautiful Love Story

Elizabeth endured hell on earth during her formative years. She was one of eleven children born to a father who was an oppressive, dictatorial tyrant. His angry rages often sent sensitive Elizabeth to her bed with any variety of ills.

It wasn't until she was forty years old that Elizabeth met Robert. He did not see her as a middle-aged invalid. Rather, he saw her as a beautiful, talented woman just waiting to blossom. Robert loved her with all his heart and withstood several brutal confrontations with Elizabeth's controlling father before he finally won her hand in marriage.

Glowing with love for each other, the couple traveled the European continent, marveling at God's wonders and at their own love. At forty-three, Elizabeth gave birth to a healthy baby.

Their lives were full and beautiful. In great joy, Elizabeth wrote to her husband the incomparable words of "How Do I Love Thee?"—perhaps the best known of her *Sonnets from the Portuguese.* True love embraced Elizabeth Barrett's life when she became Elizabeth Barrett Browning.

How Do I Love Thee?

How do I love thee? Let me count the ways.
I love thee to the depth and breadth and height
My soul can reach, when feeling out of sight
For the ends of Being and ideal Grace.
I love thee to the level of everyday's
Most quiet need, by sun and candle-light.
I love thee freely, as men strive for Right;

I love thee purely, as they turn from Praise.
I love thee with the passion put to use
In my old griefs, and with my childhood's faith.
I love thee with a love I seemed to lose
With my lost saints,—I love thee with the breath,
Smiles, tears, of all my life!—and, if God choose,
I shall but love thee better after death.

—Elizabeth Barrett Browning

Valentine's Day Around the World

In Denmark it is customary to send pressed snowdrop flowers to special friends for Valentine's Day. There is also another style of valentine that is unique to the Danes called the *gaekkebrev*, or joking letter. A male suitor writes an original rhyme, signing the letter with a code of dots only. Each dot stands for a different letter of his name. If the recipient is able to decipher the code, the suitor rewards the young lady with an Easter egg on the following Easter.

Now here is my greeting which I am writing with my own hand, as I do at the end of all my letters, for proof that it really is from me. This is in my own handwriting. May the blessing of our Lord Jesus Christ be upon you all.

2 Thessalonians 3:17–18 TLB

A Note from Me to You

Thank you for all the things you do. Sometimes with the busyness of everyday life, I forget to let you know how much I appreciate your contribution to our lives. Without you there are so many things that would be left undone, and I don't take that for granted.

Love

94

I always thank God for you because of
his grace given you in Christ Jesus.

1 Corinthians 1:4

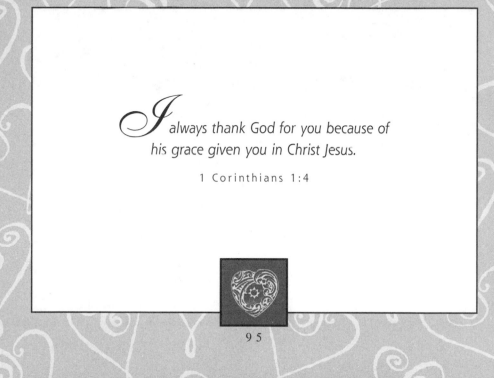

How to Make a Lace Doily Valentine

Remember making paper snowflakes? Well this project works in a similar way. Fold a rectangular sheet of white paper in quarters. Snip off the corner that has the double fold, and make "V"-shaped and half-heart cutouts along the folded edges for diamond and heart designs. Small cutouts placed close together produce the nicest effect. Cut a fancy edge along the other two sides of the paper. Make two more folds in the paper and cut out various shaped designs.

Unfold the doily, use a pin to punch tiny holes in a border around the cutouts and also punch tiny "hole" hearts and shapes in the blank areas on the white paper. When finished, paste the doily onto a sheet of red or pink paper. Continue decorating the valentine with glitter, stickers, or other adornments. Write a little message or poem and send it to the one you love!

Did you know?

The Romans believed that the heart contained the soul.
Hence began the heart to symbolize love.

A kind heart is a fountain of gladness,
making everything in its vicinity to freshen into smiles.

—Washington Irving

♥ ♥ ♥

O Lord, I will praise you with all my
heart, and tell everyone about the
marvelous things you do.

Psalm 9:1 TLB

A Sonnet for Valentine's Day

Let me not to the marriage of true minds
Admit impediments. Love is not love
Which alters when it alteration finds,
Or bends with the remover to remove:
O no! it is an ever-fixed mark
That looks on tempests and is never shaken;
It is the star to every wandering bark,

Whose worth's unknown, although his height be taken.
Love's not Time's fool, though rosy lips and cheeks
Within his bending sickle's compass come:
Love alters not with his brief hours and weeks,
But bears it out even to the edge of doom.
If this be error and upon me proved,
I never writ, nor no man ever loved.

—William Shakespeare

The First Fluttering of Love's Wings

There is nothing holier in this life of ours
than the first consciousness of love—
the first fluttering of its silken wings—
the first rising sound and breath of that wind
which is so soon to sweep through the soul,
to purify or to destroy.

—Henry Wadsworth Longfellow

*Awake, north wind,
and come, south wind!
Blow on my garden,
that its fragrance may spread abroad.
Let my lover come into his garden
and taste its choice fruits.*

Song of Songs 4:16

Love

How to Make a Valentine Cake

You will need one round cake pan and one square cake pan. The diameter of the round pan must be the same length as the sides of the square pan. Prepare your intended's favorite cake recipe, dividing the batter between the two pans. Red Velvet cake would be a fine choice with its red batter and white cream-cheese icing. Bake the cake according to its recipe.

When thoroughly cool, cut the round half of the cake into two equal parts. Place the straight side of one of the semicircles next to one side of the cake from the square pan. Place the other half of the semicircle next to an adjacent side of the square half. Insert toothpicks to connect and hold the pieces together, and ice according to the recipe. For an added touch, decorate the iced cake with red-hot candy or other red, pink, or heart-shaped confections.

Did you know?

A possible origin of Valentine's Day cards came
from Germany where cards called *freundschaftkarten*,
or friend cards, were given on New Year's Day,
birthdays, and anniversaries. In the 1700s,
the English and the Americans adopted the practice, adding
Valentine's Day to the list of important card-giving occasions.

Love

A mirror reflects a man's face,
but what he is really like is shown
by the kind of friends he chooses.

Proverbs 27:19 TLB

Submitting to One Another

Honor Christ by submitting to each other.
A man must love his wife as a part of himself;
and the wife must see to it that she
deeply respects her husband—obeying,
praising and honoring him.

Ephesians 5:21, 33 TLB

Intertwined

The man's courage is loved by the woman,
whose fortitude again is coveted by the man.
His vigorous intellect is answered by
her infallible tact. Can it be true, as is
so constantly affirmed, that there is
no sex in souls? I doubt it exceedingly.

—Samuel Taylor Coleridge

First Love

I ne'er was struck before that hour
With love so sudden and so sweet,
Her face it bloomed like a sweet flower
And stole my heart away complete.
My face turned pale as deadly pale,
My legs refused to walk away,
And when she looked, what could I ail?
My life and all seemed turned to clay.

And then my blood rushed to my face
And took my eyesight quite away,
The trees and bushes round the place
Seemed midnight at noonday.

I could not see a single thing,
Words from my eyes did start—
They spoke as chords do from the string,
And blood burnt round my heart.

Are flowers the winter's choice?
Is love's bed always snow?
She seemed to hear my silent voice,
Not love's appeals to know.
I never saw so sweet a face
As that I stood before.
My heart has left its dwelling-place
And can return no more.

—John Clare

Valentine's Day Around the World

In Wales, wooden "love spoons" were carved
and given as gifts for Valentine's Day.
Popular designs included hearts, keys,
and keyholes, signifying that the recipient
had unlocked the heart of the giver.

*T*he heart of a good man is the sanctuary
of God in this world.

—Madame Neckar

*He is my strength, my shield from every danger.
I trusted in him, and he helped me. Joy rises in
my heart until I burst out in songs of praise to him.*

Psalm 28:7 TLB

113

A Note from Me to You

Did you know that I am praying for you? I pray that all your needs will be met. I pray God will grant you the desires of your heart. I pray that He will give His angels charge over you, to keep you safe in all your ways. I pray that He will bless you as you come in and as you go out. I pray that you will know His voice and follow in His ways. I pray that goodness and mercy will follow you all the days of your life and that you will dwell in the house of the Lord forever. Amen.

*P*rayer is a sincere, sensible, affectionate pouring out of the soul to God, through Christ, in the strength and assistance of the Spirit, for such things as God has promised.

—John Bunyan

♥ ♥ ♥

The prayer of the righteous is powerful and effective.

James 5:16 NRSV

Paradise on Earth

The heart of him who truly loves
is a paradise on earth;
he has God in himself,
for God is love.

—Abbé Hugo Félicité de Lamennais

ow very good and pleasant it is
when kindred live together in unity!
It is like the dew of Hermon,
which falls on the mountains of Zion.
For there the LORD ordained his blessing,
life forevermore.

Psalm 133:1, 3 NRSV

A Love Story from the Bible

Listen! My lover! Look! Here he comes,
leaping across the mountains, bounding over the hills.
My lover is like a gazelle or a young stag.
Look! There he stands behind our wall,
gazing through the windows, peering through the lattice.

My dove in the clefts of the rock, in the hiding places
on the mountainside, show me your face,

let me hear your voice; for your voice is sweet,
and your face is lovely.

My lover is mine and I am his; he browses among the lilies.
Until the day breaks and the shadows flee,
turn, my lover, and be like a gazelle
or like a young stag on the rugged hills.

Song of Songs 2:8-9, 14, 16-17

Love

A Red, Red Rose

O my luve's like a red, red rose.
That's newly sprung in June;
O my luve's like a melodie
That's sweetly play'd in tune.

As fair art thou, my bonnie lass,
So deep in luve am I;
And I will luve thee still, my Dear,
Till a'the seas gang dry.

Till a' the seas gang dry, my Dear,
And the rocks melt wi' the sun:
I will luve thee still, my Dear,
While the sands o'life shall run.

And fare thee weel my only Luve!
And fare thee weel a while!
And I will come again, my Luve,
Tho' it were ten thousand mile!

—Robert Burns

The Kindest and Happiest Pair

The kindest and the happiest pair
will find occasion to forbear;
and something, every day they live,
to pity and perhaps forgive.

—William Cowper

Love

*Rejoice with those who rejoice;
mourn with those who mourn.
Live in harmony with one another.*

Romans 12:15–16

Did you know?

It is said that in the 1700s, young men and ladies met in the "homes of the gentry" on the eve of Valentine's Day for a social gathering. Each young man would draw a name of one the young ladies out of a hat. Then for several days, the gentlemen would wear the slips of paper on their sleeves; hence the expression, "He wears his heart on his sleeve."

*I am my lover's and my lover is mine;
he browses among the lilies.*

Song of Songs 6:3

Love Covers

Condescend to all weaknesses and
infirmities of your fellow creatures,
cover their frailties, love their excellencies,
encourage their virtues, relieve their wants,
rejoice in their friendship, overlook their unkindess,
forgive their malice,
and condescend to do the lowest offices
to the lowest of mankind.

—William Law

Above all, love each other deeply,
because love covers over a multitude of sins.

1 Peter 4:8

A Love Story from the Bible

One day Abraham said to his . . . servant, ". . . Go . . .
to my homeland . . . and find a wife for [Isaac] there."

[The servant] journeyed to Iraq. . . . [and] prayed, ". . . the girls of
the village are coming out to draw water. . . . When I ask one of them
for a drink and she says, 'Yes, certainly, and I will water your camels
too!'—let her be the one you have appointed as Isaac's wife. . . ."

As he was still speaking . . . , a beautiful young girl named
Rebekah arrived . . . . The servant asked her for a drink.
"Certainly, sir," she said . . . "I'll draw water for your camels, too."

One evening as [Isaac] was taking a walk out in the fields,
meditating, he looked up and saw the camels coming.
Rebekah noticed him and quickly dismounted. "Who is that man
walking through the fields to meet us?" she asked the servant.
And he replied, "It is my master's son!" So she covered her face
with her veil. Then the servant told Isaac the whole story. And
Isaac brought Rebekah into his mother's tent, and she became his wife.
He loved her very much, and she was a special comfort to him.

Genesis 24:2-4, 10-14, 15–19, 63–67 TLB

The happiness of married life
depends upon making small sacrifices
with readiness and cheerfulness.

—John Selden

Just for You

Breakfast in bed
consisting of your favorite morning beverage
and a muffin or bagel of your choice.

*I will sing of your strength,
in the morning I will sing of your love;
for you are my fortress.*

Psalm 59:16

132

Just for You

A fifteen-minute foot massage.

[Coupon Page]

*[Jesus] poured water into a basin and began
to wash his disciples' feet, drying them with
the towel that was wrapped around him.*

*"Now that I, your Lord and Teacher, have washed
your feet, you also should wash one another's feet."*

John 13:5, 14

Just for You

A day of enjoying your favorite hobby.

*This is the day the L*ORD *has made;*
let us rejoice and be glad in it.

Psalm 118:24

[Coupon Page]

Just for You

A walk together at your favorite scenic point.

*Glorify the LORD with me;
let us exalt his name together.*

Psalm 34:3

Just for You

A thirty-minute back massage.

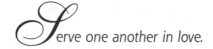

Serve one another in love.

Galatians 5:13

Just for You

Dinner at your favorite restaurant.

He has taken me to the banquet hall,
and his banner over me is love.
Strengthen me with raisins,
refresh me with apples,
for I am faint with love.

Song of Songs 2:4–5

Just for You

A date to the movie of your choice.

My lover spoke and said to me,
"Arise, my darling,
my beautiful one, and come with me."

Song of Songs 2:10

Just for You

A picnic for two.

*My beloved is a bouquet of flowers
in the gardens of Engedi.
How beautiful you are, my love, how beautiful!
Your eyes are soft as doves'.
What a lovely, pleasant thing you are, lying here upon the grass,
shaded by the cedar trees and firs.*

Song of Solomon 1:14–17 TLB

Just for You

A night together away from home and without children.
I will make all the arrangements.

May your fountain be blessed, and may you rejoice in the wife of your youth.

Proverbs 5:18

Just for You

A date at the theater or at home to
watch a romantic comedy together.
Includes popcorn or your favorite snack.

*There is a time for everything,
and a season for every activity under heaven: . . .
a time weep and a time to laugh.*

Ecclesiastes 3:1,4

Just for You

A prayer time together,
praying for the matter most
pressing in your heart.

*"I tell you that if two of you on earth
agree about anything you ask for,
it will be done for you by my Father in heaven.
For where two or three come together in my name,
there am I with them."*

Matthew 18:19–20

Love

Just for You

A candlelight dinner at home, consisting of either
your favorite meal prepared by your sweetheart
or takeout from the restaurant of your choice.

*While the king was at his table,
my perfume spread its fragrance.
My lover is to me a sachet of myrrh
resting between my breasts.*

Song of Songs 1:12–13

Just for You

A day of togetherness,
doing whatever *you* want do.

*Love each other with genuine affection,
and take delight in honoring each other.*

Romans 12:10 NLT

156

References

Acknowledgments

We acknowledge and thank the following people for the quotes used in this book:
Joseph Addison (46); Christian Nestell Bovee (22, 35); Elizabeth Barrett Browning
(91); Robert Browning (50); Edward George Bulwer-Lytton (44); John Bunyan (115);
Robert Burns (32, 117); Geoffrey Chaucer (68); John Clare (111); Samuel Taylor
Coleridge (109); Caleb C. Colton (26); Hugh Conway (15); William Cowper (122);
William Henry Davis (40); Abbé Hugo Félicité de Lamennais (120); Amantine Lucile
Aurore Dudevant (55); George Eliot (60, 80); Thomas C. Haliburton (17, 58;) Henry
Home (37); Jeremiah Brown Howell (56); Victor Hugo (63); Washington Irving (99);
Jean Baptiste Alphonse Karr (13, 82); Reverend Frances Kilvert (25); John Caspar
Lavater (39); William Law (126); Henry Wadsworth Longfellow (104); Thomas Lovell
(33); Thomas Middleton (84); John Milton (27); Thomas Moore (77); Johann Georg
Nägeli (71); Madame Neckar (113); John Bowyer Buchanan Nichols (28);John Boyle
O'Reilly (66); Jean Paul Richter (51); Sir Walter Scott (70); John Selden (130);
William Shakespeare (101); Lydia H. Sigourney (59); Robert South (42); Sir William
Temple (7); Henry Theodore Tuckerman (78); Sir Hugh Walpole (10); Henry Ware
(19); Noah Webster (20).

Additional copies of this book and other titles from Honor Books
are available from your local bookstore.
Look for the following titles throughout the season:

Happy Easter
Happy Mother's Day
Happy Father's Day
Merry Christmas

If you have enjoyed this book, or if it has impacted your life,
we would like to hear from you.

Please contact us at:
Honor Books
Department E
P.O. Box 55388
Tulsa, Oklahoma 74155
Or by e-mail at *info@honorbooks.com*